salmonpoetry40

Publishing Irish & International Poetry Since 1981

the arts council
an chomhairle ealaíon
funding literature
artscouncil.ie

the men I keep under my bed

alvy carragher

Published in 2021 by
Salmon Poetry
Cliffs of Moher, County Clare, Ireland
Website: www.salmonpoetry.com
Email: info@salmonpoetry.com

ISBN 978-1-912561-27-8

Cover Image: *Jacob Stack*
Cover Design & Typesetting: *Siobhán Hutson*

Printed in Ireland by Sprint Print

Salmon Poetry gratefully acknowledges the support of
The Arts Council / An Chomhairle Ealaíon

For Stephen Murphy
who looks at stars
and really sees them

Acknowledgements

There are many who will not be mentioned by name here. I tried to keep this to those who have read, commented on, and directly contributed to this particular book. Firstly, thanks to Jessie Lendennie, Siobhán Hutson (and all at Salmon Poetry) for your continued support. A massive thanks to Jacob Stack for the incredible cover art, I couldn't be happier with it. I want to thank Amanda Bell for a keen eye to detail during the copy edit phase.

Thanks are also due as an extract of this poem was previously featured in the *Poetry Ireland Review* with an introduction by Eavan Boland. Another excerpt appeared in *The Broken Spiral*, which was edited by R.M. Clarke. A passage also appeared in *Flare*, so thank you to Éamon Mag Uidhir. Changes have been made to these excerpts since.

Thank you to Stephen Murphy, Anne Tannam, and Fiona Bolger, all who provided extensive notes and read various drafts of this manuscript. Thanks to Mahsa Ebadpour, Lynn Harding, Jane Bulfin, Sean Scully, Lucy Carragher, Sarah Miller, Nancy Jane Bulfin, Ola Kubiak, and Ronan Daly. All have read parts of this manuscript or offered support.

Thanks to Mike McCormack for trusting me with a class at NUIG, and to that class (Leah Keane, Laura Enright, Daniel Galvin, Daniel Mulcahy, Sarah Kelly, and Megan Morrissey), this book was inspired by the honesty you brought to your work during those Friday morning workshops. I learnt a lot from each of you. I hope you all keep writing. I would also like to thank Poetry Ireland, Kevin Higgins and Susan Millar DuMars of Over the Edge, the Dublin Writers' Forum, and the Irish writing community for their continued support and encouragement.

Please note:

This is a work of fiction.

the day after (part one)

"I buried my father underground.
Since then, my ladders
only climb down,
and all the earth has become a house
whose rooms are the hours, whose doors
stand open at evening, receiving
guest after guest."

(Li-Young Lee)

1

out the door, down the stack of steps

September dark and street lights lead me along the North Circular Road
slow at first, easing myself into it, limbs stiff and dissatisfied from
lack of sleep

my runners slap the pavement
6 am cars slug by in a blur of light
my breath is a cloud to run through

I argue

part of me would like to turn around
push my key into the lock, go back indoors
melt butter into toast, brew some coffee

in that version of events, I do something wholesome
one of those activities Edi suggested like yoga
she tutted when I told her about the running
bent over, leaning forward
tapping my kneecap with her finger

"what about your knees, aren't they going to hurt"

I shrugged, always the shrug
the half-answer to uncomfy questions
I rarely consider the fate of my knees
or any of the advice Edi gives me

two minutes into the run
Phoenix Park sits, white gates against the dark

I will myself to think like an apple
which is to *grow and be and fall*
I read it in some mindfulness book, that
and a chapter about pretending to be a seed
but I don't feel seed-like, they're all untapped potential
that's the kind of metaphor Mrs Ryan loved

compare yourself to fruit

a Leaving Cert English teacher's idea of poetry
then university professors go salivating over fertile pomegranates
until we're all products of poor metaphorical training

a stitch develops, nestled in my ribs, I slow
focus on filling up my lungs

half a mile into the park
the Garda Barracks to my back
I take the boring road
one flat line out to the trails
I snake along the border walls
save the hills for when I'm tired
for when the effort matters

eleven minutes in, too soon to go back

when I run, I think of Scott Jurek
foot bandaged, suffering across Death Valley
I tried his technique before, shortening steps
increasing turnover, it felt treadmill heavy

(I should stop reading about Scott, he subsists on rice balls)

the length of a stride
feels like my body yawning across the ground
waking itself up

the grass that lines the road is wet and leaning
it smells like rain has been and rain is coming

I wear thin gloves
an old cotton race t-shirt, ratty leggings
the t-shirt has *I've been to Hell & Back* scrawled across it

if rain comes, cold will crawl into my lungs
make itself at home, spend weeks escaping through my nose
that's if I don't get gutted by a deer first, splatted by a car

I always scare myself with death

I'll run a little further
I don't want to deal with him
I'll have to ask him to leave
or make him breakfast
let him leave without a fuss

I'm good at pretending
smile, chit chat, then after he leaves
never reply to any texts
assuming he's the sort to text

I need to find his Facebook page, he must have one
that way I can check where he's likely to show up
and avoid all those places

ah, this is my favourite bit
the dark is softer now
trees stretch toward the last chunk of moon

the moon will be gone
by the time I turn to go home
the sun will be coming up in front of me
its low-slung glow forcing me to watch the trail closely

I cross the back of the park
consider going further
but I can't miss the bus

it's best to act normal

people do this all the time, it's nothing to feel anything about
I need to stop being whimsical, me and my romantic notions

I'll veer here, loop through the wood
come out in front of the Ambassador's Residence
I love that stretchy piece of grass
it goes on for miles, deer skirt its edges

once a desolate woman stopped me
about half a mile into the park

"they said there were deer, do you know where"

I told her to keep going, they go wherever they like
she was wearing stupid shoes, I doubt she went any further
but you won't just stumble on beauty, it doesn't hang around
waiting

maybe he'll be gone by the time I get back
what was I thinking, I wasn't thinking, not really

is that a valid excuse for acting the mouldy slut

I push the thought back

it's not very feminist to consider myself a mouldy slut
I've agency over my body and all that 21st-century shite

there's the road again
return across the trails or down the main road
that cuts through the centre of the park

I don't want to ruin the trail by associating it with this morning

I must be careful when I'm fragile
a subtle stump of wood
might stick in my subconscious

then months later
when I'm the new me
I'll take that trail
notice Stumpy and
it will all come back
as if it never got put away

the road is spotted with the odd runner now
morning-time soul-searchers

cars slip into the city

I slow again, come close to stopping
the thud of dehydrated head hurt
I'll glug a pint of water, painkillers

recover from this ritual of pain

in six months, I've not learnt that
Dublin isn't kind

one glass becomes five
each glass a reminder that
I'm worn out by it all

it's okay for Sarah, Fridays start late for her
blundering out of bed at 11 am
right about the time I slot into my desk
down my first coffee

it's hard to resist her, I tried

"ah come on Beth
Diarmaid is driving me mad
would you not go for one
it'll do you good to get back out there"

thirty minutes, almost home

a man practices tai chi between the trees
a strange place to be at peace, so near the road
but I suppose the trick is finding peace there anyway

people can't seem to keep calmness to themselves
it seeps out of their pores, gets right up in my face
asks why I'm ticking over a thousand thoughts

up around the Polo Grounds
a runner strides on the other side of the grass

I pick the pace up, not slogging, not me
my stomach lumps at the new tempo

the tall thin loping figure goes by
I give him the runner's nod
once his footfalls are out of earshot
I slow to a waddle

I can't do this

the zoo's green fence holds in the sound of animals
their morning chorus, strangely haunting

how weak I am
the slower pace brings him back to me

I hope he's not asleep
that he got up, slipped out, left no note
so I can romanticise

what if

I hadn't gone running
left him slumped across my sheets

it's unsettling to watch a stranger sleeping
to feel their weight pressed along me in the bed
to see how vulnerable they can be in my presence
or how they reach towards me in their sleep
me or some memory of a girl

it is she they clutch at before waking

once awake
they realise she is gone

once awake
there is stilted conversation
or half-baked sex
to fill the not knowing
the mutual not wanting to know

this man was no sleep-reacher
not the sort to get hung up on hauntings
he was the nightmare of first attempts
rough and quick and rolled over

he left me wet and wanting

I didn't ask him to leave
I let him sleep

by morning, his light snore
took up all the room in my head

now, I jog alongside the barracks

a batch of gardaí set out to run

light is piecing the day together
people have that tired Friday slouch

I pass a uniformed girl with her mother
it seems sad that someone so young
is so perfectly pressed
her footsteps skip, bag jolting behind her

I should not be getting so down in the drudge
I could sleep all day Saturday

no sleep, it's Granny's birthday
I've to bus-haul home

Granny is eighty
one of those ages that seems impossible

imagine explaining to Granny that I've slept with a man
because I wanted to be held, but then he never held me

stop this, breathe, cop on

200 metres to the door
I need to quit moping
quit longing for boys that spoon
or have encyclopaedic knowledge
of random topics

I tried explaining to Sarah
about wanting someone fascinating

she asked

"but like fascinating how"

a butterfly enthusiast
someone who builds intricate watches
trains themselves to write the Japanese alphabet

Sarah says

"that is the definition of being too fussy"

I suspect the reality of a Japanese-writing butterfly enthusiast
would involve the kind of person who alphabetises their socks
sucks the last bit of chicken from the bone with a slurpy sound

creak of gate, I jog up the steps
fiddle with my keys at the door
try to remember his name
perhaps I'll need to use it

was he a Conor or maybe an accountant
I associate accountants with bland names

I push open the door
the hall is the dark of rest

I pause, before entering

2

up the carpeted stairs
trailing in leaves, dirt

it's not the kind of morning
for taking off my shoes
I'm sick of all that considering
tired of consequences
the full sweat of the run hits me
t-shirt limp from body heat

I nip into the bathroom
close the toilet, sit on its lid
elbows on knees, head in hands
what to do

in the mirror, drained, dark-eyed
no pink in my cheeks

I rise, press my nose against my reflection
cold tap gushes, I cup my palm under the flow
scoop the waterfall over my face
dip my head, lips ducked under the tap
fill my mouth, swill it around
water warms, froths

I spit out the after-taste of sweaty spit
I can't go into the bedroom like this

I tug a brush through hair
pat concealer under eyes
smudge out the dark circles
a lashing of mascara

(no harm in looking closer to my best)

there's little I can do about the outfit,
suck my stomach in, resent my impulse to be thinner

he's asleep, doesn't hear me pad across the room
I stay quiet, find my most flattering clothes
it's not that I want him to fancy me
it's more like
I cannot let him see me

the last time I wore this dress I felt
good, it dips, hugs the right places
but not today
today, it's asking me not to force it

he coughs in his sleep
a tight knot climbs up my throat

I tiptoe towards the bed
retrieve my shoes from under it
black with a kitten heel
I'll be crippled by 3 pm

stop this, brain, whisht

he rolls over in his sleep
I might escape without him waking

I reach for my fob and coat
place them on the back of the chair
before going to the kitchen

*

Sarah is sitting at the table
more dressing gown than human
face resting on her arms

she jumps when I enter

"so"

'shouldn't you be in bed'

"well yeah
but I wasn't going to wait all day for the news
so, did you"

'did I what'

I'm whispering

the idea of him hearing is too much
the idea of him waking is too much

"you know"

there's a smirk on her face
Sarah wants to be single

'yeah'

"and"

'nothing special'

"well the first time is never"

'yeah'

this will wait

'I'll tell you later, I'm late
I've work'

*"oh right, well I suppose
pre-coffee sex chats are not ideal"*

there's a wink in her voice

'yeah, I'll be good and
caffeinated by tonight'

"will I get a bottle"

I'm about to say no, when out comes a yes
isn't that always the fucking way with me

*

in the bedroom, he has woken
gangly and naked
taking up more space than before
no longer curled into his sleep
pulling a t-shirt over his head
the dark brown curls of his chest disappear
the slight bump of his stomach gone

I stand in the door
he reaches down, checky boxers
the squares jig and blur

'you're up'

I want to say
it is morning, can you go, what's your name, why did you stay,
do you've any manners
you're not expecting breakfast, are you, how does this
keep happening to me

but none of the words make it out

"I am, yeah"

all casual lean, zipping up his jeans
giving me the once over
the sizing up, the decision
about whether he got lucky or not
if I'm worth boasting about

'that's good'

eyes stuck to my work fob
slung across the chair

'I've work'

I give him one of Mammy's sure what can you do looks
the one she uses when she's no energy left to argue

"well I, eh, can I've your number"

he asks
but it's not a real question
the modern-day equivalent of etiquette
like asking a lady for a second dance
but bailing before the third
(the eighties in the midlands
according to my mother)

from the way he asked
he will never use the number

unless drunk, unless 3 am
unless desperate and lonely
unless Tinderless

I give it to him deadpan
let the sound fill up the room

"sound, I'll give you a text"

he tucks the phone into his pocket

I gesture towards the door
I do not want him, but it hurts to be rejected

he got what he came for
maybe I'm just bad at this

he gives me a cold kiss on the cheek
the kind offered up to dead people
forced out for grannies

he is gone

a minute later, Sarah is in the room

"jesus the state of the place
what were yee up to at all"

she indicates my clothes, scattered across the floor

"he was all right
if Diarmaid didn't have me nailed down
you'd be in for a bit of competition"

she moves to sit on the bed

'I should be gone already
tonight, yeah'

"pull a sickie, sure it's Friday
you'll do fuck all in there with the head on ya"

'that would be the third this month
how would I explain'

"the horrors of flu season"

'I'm out the door'

"I'll be right here when you get back"

I force out a laugh
rush down the steps

3

rain gives our road a soggy air
I step into it, cold, fresh

hood down to soak my hair
nobody will see the grease then
I'll say I was destroyed by the rain
easier than the truth

cars are angry by 8 am
backed up and beeping
radios and sleep-driving

a cyclist slogs up the hill towards me
collides with a woman crossing the road
she lies on the tarmac stunned, he curses

she apologises
sorry, sorry, sorry

I want to say
it's not your fault, screw the bastard

someone blares their horn
nobody asks if she's okay

typical

that word blooms in my head

typical

typical men

when I take a man
and hold him in the pillow of my body
I round some internal corner
feel my love revert to childhood

enough, stop brain, stop

focus, there
the trees drip offerings
nature's smallest prayers

remember
my life is heavy with privilege
the world is full of refugees
dictators, fences, walls

Dublin is a city of bridges not fences
each arched across the water
each promising more than it gives

glance left along this very road
the outline of high-rise flats
the red brick of trouble
each home slapped on top of another

Parkgate Street's bin bags stand to notice

this is a late-night street, a drink and devil pavement
I've waltzed it enough times, holding enough hands

I list my hours, spreadsheets, calls to make
in this work-prep blur, I shove my way on to the Luas
we drip one slow puddle, making eye contact with the floor

the city has taught me
to tuck my eyes away, to stop looking

at first, I practiced the waves of country living
but eyes skip over and through you

it's a gift of survival
how to see without looking
how to look and not notice
we clutch the yellow bars
fingers almost, but not quite, bumping

I stand in the armpit of a suited man
(I let strangers pump me
but shudder over public-transport pit action)

snot-clogged sniffs, the hum of the Luas
the smell of damp bodies, anonymous morning farting
a commercial Irish accent naming stops
with each stop, more of the rain traipses in

*

I hurry down a side street to the bus stop
but the bus is slashing puddles at those who've missed it
another in ten minutes

I tuck in beside the Polish Embassy door
a wheelie bin beside me, shiny black with rain
a downpour does the city good

Edi wouldn't agree
apparently Dublin is unsalvageable, she never visits
because her shaman said it interrupts her energy

our coffees last hours
it is always the same
the shadow of our father

once, she told me about the shaman
every three months he pulls out the shadow from her stomach
she demonstrated, arms tugging at some invisible rope

"in the morning
I felt so light"

but it grew-up inside her, came back angrier than before
because it knew she was trying to forget

*

"can you spare two euro love, I'm not drinking"

his breath is whiskey-laced against my face
cornered, the wet of wheelie bin slides down my leg

here again, plugged into some other universe
caught space-eyed and absent from my head

'I've no change'

he presses on
I didn't mean to make him beg
I finger the change in my pocket

"I need two euro to get back to Mullingar love
I swear to God, would I lie to you love"

I want to say
yes, you would lie to me, I'm nobody to you
you've lied to people you love
I smell it on you, it's in the shake of your shoulders
I'm sorry but can you take two steps back

instead, out parades a predictable *sorry*
he sees me for who I really am, turns away

*

the bus arrives, the Swords Express
we lumber towards it
stepping out from under doorways
shuffle, step, shuffle, beep, shuffle, step, shuffle

comfort in the rhythm of people finding seats
I close my eyes against the morning
let it simply be a sound that surrounds me
the chatter warmed by different accents

"ah, but my best friend, he break the girlfriend
so I've to spend the night with him"

"what about you, will you be at the Christmas party"

"Barry will get the promotion
he was in the meeting for forty-five minutes
the fucker wouldn't even tell me what they said like"

"ah no, I went to the pub, it was too wet
the rain it gets in the way of my fitness"

"but she was like such a bitch about it"

"maybe I'll take next Friday off
I hate Fridays
I would like to be somewhere else"

that's just it, isn't it
we would all like to be somewhere else

4

at Airside Central, the bus shudders to a stop
an American transplant on Dublin's outskirts
paved and grey and glass
McDonalds, TGI Fridays, Starbucks
one dodgy nightclub sits between them
dress Dublin up with chrome-lined business parks
but a dank dance floor still crouches nearby
where drunk teenagers totter in stilettos

pure drudgery
like this line, dressed dull as slugs
making its way into office buildings

I'm at the back, they group, giggle

ahead is Eva, who I've never met
one long silhouette of woman
there is usually some man repeating her name
as often as possible

once or twice
I've passed her long skirt
as she waits for the bus alone
wondered if I should mutter hello
if we'd have stuff in common

"Eva, I've to ask, why are you following me"

this runt of a man is flirting
she offers up a smile, no words
perhaps those are kept sacred

"Eva, Eva, I think you are teasing me, what do you think"

he addresses Eva's squat friend

"is Eva sad today"

squat laughs

but none of her body is in it
forced to hide her understanding
of her place in the conversation

the laugh is like Mammy's
at the table, tired from digging her garden
Edi and I were six and seven

light cottage-dim, he entered

on the floor, we tried to jigsaw more quietly
waited to see who he would pick
breath held
between our hearts and necks

Mammy didn't look up
(her mistake)
head rested on a hand
propped up by her elbow
a face that needed sleep

"your elbow is on the table"

the air tightened around us
Mammy lifted her head
(absentmindedly)

"look at Mammy, girls
no better than the rest of us
with her elbows on the table
laugh at her"

we did
relieved it wasn't us this time
pointed, laughed, mocked

Mammy didn't cry
but you could tell she wanted to

out came one painful tired laugh

she once said it broke her heart
three pairs of the same eyes turned against her

I hate this
my father shows up
when I least expect him

fold him away

I've spent enough of today
on men who don't love me

*

Eva disappears into an office
I march towards mine

cars sit into parking spaces, coats tight against the drizzle
one melodramatic suit legs it with a file held over his head
barging past me, moving with the conviction of his own
importance

I shuffle-push through the door
Niamh is slotted into reception
terminally cheerful

"Beth, good morning, I got you a latte
thought you might need one"

it is perched on my desk

"it's caramel cos it's friiiiday
a bitta sugar to celebrate"

'aw Niamh you shouldn't have
you're too good'

"I'm off to do the rounds
make sure nobody runs out of biros
y'know yourself, I'll drop the post up"

'I'll hold down the fort'

I sound like my mother
I paste her on for workdays
act as if what we do matters

I nod, smile, furrow
on demand
catchphrases include

sure, isn't that terrible

ah jesus, you must be having me on

I give the world exactly what it expects
which is to say, not much

I sip the *latte*, press it to my face
let it warm my cheek
as the computer boots up

eight-hour days spent
helloing their toing and froing
I know the sound of their footsteps

here's Brad, a nervy step, squeaky shoes
some wife-related drivel, a receding hairline

next Mark, sloughing across the ground
makes glib comments about the weather

Leah bounds and bounces
full of some theatre production from last night

Karen comes with precise footsteps

"did you perhaps notice that there's no milk"

'I'm only just in Karen
I haven't had a minute'

"I see"

tone suggesting she doesn't

*"would it be fair to assume
the milk was running low last night"*

'I guess'

"to be clear, I'm not implying it's your fault
but correct me if I'm wrong"

a smile so skinny it's almost not there

"monitoring the milk situation
isn't that one of your duties"

'I suppose'

I fold my arms, stare
at her over-plucked, underlined eyebrows

"well I mean"

her teeth are finding it hard not to gloat their way out of her mouth

"then I'm not sure what the issue is"

'neither am I'

"the milk"

her tone is clipped

I want to say
he makes you so miserable
why do you let him, anyone who listens
can hear the undertone of heartbreak
a more efficient milk-supply will not
stop him breathing in your ear at night

'what Karen
will I go and get some
all you've to do is ask'

if Karen could kill me, she would
(a more complete version of Karen would kill most people)
she marches away

I sit back
text Niamh to pick up milk
we barter over excuses to leave the building

I adjust my seat
let emails flit across my screen
spam, spam, stationery order, spam, spam

my schedule allows half an hour for this
I could slide my eyes across the orders
spend time crafting responses
perhaps that's what all this time is for
they don't want skim readers
knee-jerk responders typing

no problem, let me know
if you need anything else

I swivel in the seat
switch on the giant plasma screen TV
people rarely watch it, but sometimes I stare at it for hours
willing the minutes to move across the screen
hoping whatever bloated politician is speaking at me
will swallow time, let it sink down inside their giant mouth
tongue pushing it forward
past morning air-conditioning rants

"it's fucking freezing in my cubicle, would you not put the heating on"

"I'm sweating buckets up there, it's not even winter yet"

back and forward to the air-conditioning controls
up one degree on floor three in the right-hand corner
where Matilda is typing from under a pile of coats
down two degrees on the second floor
where David's armpit secretions are impacting office productivity

pushing further still
past Niamh's commentary on Emmerdale
DHL delivery men talking about the weather

time pauses briefly for Edna, the post lady
who shows us a picture of her wedding dress
says her daughter has started speaking
gives us both a smile

"don't let them get you down"

Niamh laughs at the idea of being down

"go away with you, sure we've it easy"

we do
by 11 am's coffee top-up
we've solved the mystery of the missing staples
placed an order for silent sellotape

or as Karen explained

"tape that shows consideration for others"

we sign in a wrinkled suit
he leans in over our desk

"what are two pretty girls like you
doing in a place like this"

I want to say
we are sitting, what does it look like
and you sir, do you do much beyond leer
do you want to hear our delicate intricacies

I know you, in a way that you will never know me
because you are staring at my hair, my breasts, my eyes

you don't see my leg shake as you ask some other question
you've not heard my voice when it's pitched quiet, low, its actual sound
not this complex girlish noise that comes out over telephones
and for you, it stands to attention around men like you

Niamh is better at these situations
she fixes-him-up with the kind of sugar
passed down to her by other women

like a recipe for Granny's gingerbread
or the secret to fashioning the perfect tart
the one that saw them all through marriage

"aren't you an old charmer
if I was twenty years older"

that is, she says no
but keeps it harmless
she offers him the desire he wants
without the humiliation he deserves

I bite my lip
without the guts to do either

he has the stooped shoulders of my grandfather
old eyes, you can read twinkles into them or sad stories

because of this, I stay silent
like I do with grandad
who walks circles through his bungalow

sometimes he hears her in the bedroom

John, I'm listening, John, I'm watching, John, I'll always love you

gone three years
how those years have changed him
stooped over ancient mythology
drinking almond milk
he says she sends messages
through a flickering lightbulb

some days, he times the darkness
sends my father updates on its frequency

then my father phones me
as if no generation can kill the ghosts of the last
as if we're all buried with them
and their dirt is trapped between our teeth
forming the sleep in our eyes

5

Niamh puts on nail polish
under the desk
one finger at a time
so as not to draw suspicion

I've let him itch all day
refused to examine him
hold him up to Niamh's light

I don't need her opinion
smile a little tight as she
examines the facts

that word coming out heavy-handed

pet

not meaning harm by it
but managing it anyway

(isn't that always the way)

Daddy used to call us pet on good days, *slut* on bad ones
both words reduce me to my four-foot self
so that *slut* has the ring of love about it
and *pet* sounds ominous

*

after lunch, Niamh says

*"why the sour puss
did you miss me that much"*

a recurring joke, her daily dig
to remind me about smiling

there have been complaints from visiting guests
about my inability to convey enthusiasm

I'm inclined to agree, it's hard not to
when you consider their troubles

"no you can't have my name
tell him I'm here, he's expecting me"

"there's a wet patch on the floor
I could kill myself, you should get a sign at least"

"what is it you do exactly
it must be nice, sitting there all day"

if I die
the milk and stationery will stop
until they plug-in another graduate
who hasn't been brave enough to leave

most of my friends are gone
the rest are planning departures
Melbourne, Sydney, Dubai, Vancouver, New York
half our parish ended up in London

on Sunday mornings
they post pictures that could have been taken in Roscrea
six years ago, all the same drunk expressions
these days, they've ditched GAA shirts for proper jumpers

some days, I research flights, visas
a new life across an ocean
but I'd be lonely
Skyping Edi in pidgin Irish
to give myself a sense of home
when overcome by rootlessness

Niamh is staying
she has a five-year plan
involving a mortgage

as lunch settles in our stomachs
Niamh tells me about WE
the other half of WE is HE

HE is her upside-down Claddagh ring

“WE *really didn’t like that film*
it was awful, WE *left early*”

what’s it like to be a half rather than a whole
I was half of Edi, until college

now, we are WhatsApp messages
pinging back and forth

“are you going home this weekend”

‘nah, need to catch up on sleep,
you know yourself’

“I’m going, Mammy is going mad
she could do with some company”

‘I’ll go next weekend
Daddy sent me a WEIRD text’

“why do you still talk to him”

the conversations end without goodbyes
sucked back into our separate lives

as Niamh shows me engagement rings
I check my phone, blank, blank, blank
usually Edi would have texted by now

for years
I, or Edi, or Mammy
would wake at night
cold sweat and crying
knowing it was one of the others
we would send 2 am texts asking

“are you okay”

someone would respond

“no, can I call you”

I read that the trauma of a mother
gets passed down to her daughters
like a love of lemonade or pickled cabbage
like hair that won't curl or the inability to say no

nobody sends those texts much anymore
when they do, they arrive days late

*

Niamh has enlarged an eight thousand euro ring across her screen
I am about to oohlala
when he appears

"Beth I've been trying to catch you"

normally Niamh would interrupt
but not when it comes to him
she thinks it's cute

the first time she met him, she told me

"there's a guy upstairs that runs"

I imagine she told him

"there's a girl downstairs that runs"

as if that is all it takes

when his footsteps tap across the ground
I pick up the phone, pretend to be talking
today, he has caught me unaware

last night's stranger
can-canning across my face
emblazoned on my knickers

'oh, hi'

I act surprised, as if I've no clue that he's been trying to catch me
but two weeks play through my mind of stopping to tie my shoes
head in a book at the bus stop, rifling through my bag
choreographing coffee breaks, all to avoid him

he's kind
but that's not all he is

he remembers details, insists on retelling them
as if to illustrate a theorem for caring
laughs when I'm not even shooting for funny
holds doors when I'm at the other side of a room
even when insisting to hold them becomes comical
a kind of forced behaviour

my father lives in his voice
crawls out his mouth
creeps up my arm hairs

I know what lives inside men this persistent

"I saw this book and thought you'd like it"

he presses it down on my desk
I glance at the cover

'thank you'

I don't comment further
it is the sequel to one I read last week

"so where have you been"

'right here'

Niamh plays with a strand of hair
clicks through an official looking spreadsheet

"okay, well enjoy the book, I'll catch you later"

he leaves

hands warm and clammy
I push the book to one side

'where were we'

Niamh is kind enough to leave me be
the ring reappears on her screen
we give ourselves over to its details

6

by 4 pm, we've compiled a wish list
of rings, wedding dresses and venues
including a farmer charging newlyweds to glamp
I imagine a city bride with notions about feeding pigs
clutching a hot water bottle in her sleep

Fridays allow time for this
after lunch the complaints come to an abrupt halt
everyone returns to their desks to wait out the week's final hours
floors empty out early

half an hour before close
Niamh does a security check

I clean the coffee machines
three, one on each floor
each with its own hymn
a clean-cycle involving crusted milk
and a specific set of toothbrushes

a man came to train me
wagging mini-toothbrushes in my face
stating the importance, eyeing me
as if coffee-machine maintenance was beyond me
I tried to reassure him

'I've worked in bars before'

he lengthened the lecture

"I'll tell you somethin' for nothin'
the biggest problem with machines is people
that's right, all you young lads, thinkin' you
know your arse from your bleedin' elbow"

I should have been more appalled
reported him to management
but I'm used to it

Daddy was the same
the days pot made him paranoid
hoovering the carpet became a crisis

"remove all the dirt from this room, all of it"

he would fidget
standing in a clean room

if I was dumb enough to protest
he would open cupboards
pull books from shelves
indicate dust-filmed covers
hold up a dirt-clotted finger

"do you call this clean"

'no'

"what's that"

'no'

"well then, clean it again"

and I would bend to the task for hours
dusting, hoovering, cursing Edi
if she got to play or vice versa
he was always pitting us against each other

it was best to keep him happy

happy, happy, happy
is a word, I tell myself
as I push the toothbrush in and out
of the machine's hundred corners

others enter the kitchen
relocate lunchboxes, leave

nobody stops to say hello

at reception, they all meet my eye
offer up small talk
but when they catch me
cleaning up their mess
they avert their eyes
phones slide into hands

we're all at it, forgetting the inconvenient truths
outside these walls are people who would work harder
for half my wages

toothbrushes back in pouch, rinse hands
let the tap-sprung water soothe

I head downstairs, past sleek orange chairs
plastic tables, this ultra-modern prison
stock photos of gender-balanced families
wallpapered along the halls

clunk down steps
the lights are off on the ground floor

Niamh taps her foot
fiddles with her keys
coat on, scarf snug

"what time do you call this
you'd swear we've nowhere to be"

*

the bus stop is a clogged line of scrunched coats
slow-drenching rain, patient types give up their place to shelter

I shiver-stand, weigh up dinner options
reheatable gloop, or peel real-food
mash butter into potatoes, slow-cook beef
until it breaks at the push of a wooden spoon
add onions, garlic, thyme, salt, let it simmer

most days, I eat toasted sandwiches or packet soup
chicken slapped in the oven without ornamentation
munch through half-assed salads

proper meals bring me back
Mammy showing me how to make jam
collect berries, check for wormy bastards
bad ones flung, snapped up by our dog

or the two of us, bent over a raw chicken
wet and slapped on the counter
my hand shoved up it, eyes closed
fingering the knot of giblets
scared I'd get stuck between thighs

learning to dice an onion
flatten garlic without letting
the smell get into my skin
identifying parsley's many guises
rubbing thyme to let the flavour out

two women in front of me talk
(also slaves to food's magic)

"I cook it in sugar water, not many bother
sugar water makes it taste like home"

"we eat the heart, the liver, no waste"

when Daddy was down low where he could love us
he would set a smoothie on the table
get us to guess the fruits and spices
ginger pear was a safe bet
he'd sneak in beetroot, cumin

Edi always guessed right first time
I thought it was the alchemy of her tongue
a gift I'd failed to acquire
later, she admitted to examining
the contents of the compost heap
naming the decaying peels

as a child, I thought *chef*, saw myself on cobbled streets
serving fresh coffee, cheese, pastries
food so good the taste would get stuck in your mouth

until I worked with a chef
a reddish-purple man, stressed over steaks
cooking that bland menu for forty years
cursing anyone who asked why

he died of a heart attack
face down on the grill

*

the bus arrives
we file on sluggish
there's less rattle of chat
the odd pair heading off for drinks
someone wanting to quit
another mentions a wedding

Sarah has texted

"I've started on the wine"

all I want to do is shower
curl-up in pyjama-fluff

I can still smell him on me
leftovers of his cologne
strong and branding

he is the sort that has worn the same scent
since he was sixteen, a scent the mother bought
now, his default setting

so much of what we do is done without thinking

screw it, I text Sarah back

'keep us a glass
I'll be home soon'

"not to worry, I got three bottles
do you know me at all like
I wouldn't let my BAE down x"

my mind gives over to him

his face all blurry now
the press of his hand against mine
bra disappearing before I had decided

I'm not sure

only that I was separate
somewhere above
waiting for him to finish

and I was thinking of him
not again

he comes to bed with every man I date
as if to tell me I can't have them

when I stare at ceilings
watch shadows move across the wall
or push out unconvincing sighs

Oh god because yes
is too much of an answer
and nobody asks any questions

Oh god like
the night he played Bob Dylan to me
afterwards, threw down the guitar

"I'm not a fucking puppet, I can't do this"

'I never asked you to'

I wanted to say
don't talk to me about puppets
you wear your hair and your sorrow like Dylan

he wanted a girl who made him feel like singing
what he meant was more sexually deviant

not a girl
a woman

he said he wanted a woman
my ovaries felt so insignificant

*

the bus comes to a stop
I'm not sure where the time has gone
a dark hole of memory

Edi says

"you've to try to stay present"

blowing on her tea, concerned
considering the great sadness of mindlessness

and really, what am I meant to say
I try, but I'm not very good at it

the bus is easy
I can fill in all the blanks
teenagers outside the Three Arena
bus lurching along the Liffey
traffic lights and choice words
thrown at anyone breaking them

pedestrians in shoes that are bad for their backs
office buildings releasing their inmates
and yet, if I squint into the high ones
some still tap away at endless lists

the bus driver's station of choice
Today FM claiming to have the last word
with Matt Cooper lecturing Ireland
niggle, niggle, niggle

as leftover Celtic Tigers proclaim that
employment is up, up, up

"we can't cope with the growth Matt
there's almost more jobs than people"

and in a farmhouse in County Leitrim
one of those places where jobs don't show up
some tired mother with a son in Australia
switches off the radio, puts on some eighties hits
and dances like she did before boom 'n' bust

"no use listening to it, no use at all
you'd only waste the time of your life
listening to those gobshites"

*

I plough down the three steps
into Dublin's air and sirens

head toward the Liffey
a murky black line
green gunk growing up its sides
once, they found a trunk in it
full of severed body parts
or was that the canal
I'm useless at remembering
good at assuming

the Liffey looks like a storage unit for the dead
there's a breed of people that swim down it
and afterwards, what happens
once they are home and warm and dry
do they see ghosts, or cough up algae for a week
its green sludge pooling before them

I grew up one mile from a spring
if you wanted nice water, you'd pinch a mug from the kitchen
go uphill across the fields to the mini grotto

Mary stood, peeling paint and dirty pious lips
I'd mutter a prayer before hunkering down
letting the mug sink into the clear stream

when all the water froze over
and the road was sheets of ice
we went to Mary
damp and dark and mossy
her earth untouched by frost
all around the grotto hung icicles

there are places like that
Edi calls them touched
but Edi sees fairies
full-grown women where there are none

for years, she claimed the devil lived in her wall
Daddy made it worse by agreeing
pointing at shadows and asking

"is that him"

until sleep became a skill
Edi couldn't master

*

I text Sarah

*'10 more minutes
and I'm all yours'*

it's strange to me
how capable
I am of seeming okay

even with Sarah
who has been there since thirteen
who witnessed all my awkward years
and hates my father

she's never really met him
except the day, he stood in the hall
laughing at her taste in music

*"the Beach Boys
why would anyone
listen to them"*

for Sarah that was all it took
she texts

*"I'm dyinnnnnnng
Diarmaid is after getting cake
so much for the fucking diet"*

Diarmaid would not survive Friday night
if he didn't bring the cake
that will be bloating our stomachs by midnight

*

Montpelier Hill, this road is not like it sounds
red brick and flats, children pushing prams
up and down outside their homes
one girl, three or four, sparkly leggings
arms crossed, yelling at an older sister

"I don't want to be the baby"

she won't be convinced
her mind made up
I used to be like that

at three, flinging a bonnet in the river
so I wouldn't have to wear it again

at five, casting Edi as my husband
in every game we played

*'you've to kiss me
goodbye, but I
don't want to*

touch your lips'

at seven, announcing to my mother

'you needn't buy me
dresses anymore
I won't wear them'

at eight, picking up a boy
by the scruff of his neck
for slagging my father

'you don't ever
let me hear you
speak about my daddy
like that again'

at nine, telling Edi

'Mammy doesn't love Daddy
you can ask her'

later that day, Mammy confirmed it

'well he broke my heart Edi
so, I don't love him anymore
but I love you both very, very much'

at ten, Daddy by my side
sitting in the front seat of the car
promising him

'no, I won't tell her'

at sixteen, throwing a solid wood chess board at his head

'it's not fair,
you can't do this'

at seventeen, sitting on a low garden wall with Edi

'I wish he was dead'

her answer

"yeah, me too"

since then, I've lost the ability to inhabit my convictions
they rattle through me unspoken

*

the trees of Phoenix Park shadow the road

what story should I give Sarah

maybe
there were heavy makeup girls
who wanted him, all clucking
it's the only reason I noticed him
I wanted whatever they were having

he wasn't special
maybe he works in their office
so they see beyond his rounded Irish jaw
the slight push of a beer nourished stomach

maybe, I was drunk enough and anonymous enough
for him to like the look of me

no, I won't tell her that

maybe, he came after me
across a crowded dance floor
I gave in eventually

no, not that
she won't believe me

finally, the North Circular Road
I count the houses to my own

here's the family that always seem to be outside
hanging out of windows, doors, wheelie bins
children in every inch of their space
a Despicable Me minion sits in a window
one round eye unblinking

the apartment below ours has a mobile
a lighthouse placed street-side of their net curtain
above it wooden clouds hang, fabric seagulls circle

the steps greet me, I ready myself for Sarah's questions
penis length, positions, horsing over details

inside, the long hall mirror
matted tan carpet, twist the key
Tom Waits pours out from the kitchen
I let heavy footsteps announce me

"Beth, throw your stuff in the room
then get your arse in the sitting room and have a gawk at the table
I've outdone myself, napkins! my mother rubbed off on me after all"

clanging of pots
Sarah's voice off-key
but in time with Tom's

"well I stumbled in the darkness
lost and alone"

my door hangs open
the room is back where it should be
strewn clothes have been folded

Sarah's care is in the way the bed is tucked perfectly at the corners
my patchwork blanket spread neatly out, cushions arranged the way
I like them

I lie down for a moment, ceiling-stare
I listen to her sing
the clatter of cooking

I'm so very, very tired

just

shut

my

eyes

for

a

minute

let

sleep

come

sudden

and

solid

a series of night dreams

(i)

two faceless men
ask over and over
where my father is
I repeat my answer
white wrists held forward

take me instead

(ii)

Edi and I run away
with a car stolen from our old primary school
we rob packets of Taytos, but can't open them
driving backwards down a coastal road

Edi whispers to herself

free, free, free

until we crash into a cow
then there's just mooing

(iii)

he is inside the post-box
a black-haired spider
legs thick with tight muscle
web-spread across the post

Edi tells me to *hurry*
Daddy wants the post

I poke him with a stick
the thunder of fear around me

(iv)

our attic room and Daddy's old work-shed
both places grown together, sewn with ivy

two places at once

I sit at the gap where the steps come up
legs dangling in air, above hard concrete
don't fall, a brain spasm stops me
from trying to split my head in two

going home (part two)

in childhood, I thought
that pain meant
I was not loved.
It meant I loved.

(Louise Glück)

1

I wake in one gulp

my father's face tucked under my eyelids

the bed is empty except for me
and the patchwork quilt
I took with me to college
stuffed in a suitcase made up of my mother

a Roald Dahl Treasury
a well-thumbed copy of Pride and Prejudice
and the quilt she stitched in the middle of her marriage
a sea of blues and purples
each piece its own universe of hand-stitched care
patterns going in heart-led directions
each square holds birds, leaves, spirals

I sprawl out, body as long and wide as I can make it
the blue of my dress hiked up around my stomach
I like how ungainly the morning makes me
as if in sleep my body lets itself be whatever

I peel the stick of tights from my legs, let skin breathe
roll off knickers, rub my hand over lycra lines
un-zip the side of my dress, my stomach decompresses
I struggle out of it, zip catching my hair
tug down my bra until it's a deflated loop around my stomach
lie on my back, belly letting go of all its notions

rise and fall, rounded mountain
don't shudder, I try to feel unapologetic
this should be easy, I must love all of this
I can't be blamed for it, the body of being female

concentrate on the light tickle of my eyelids
sticky with sleep, nudge into their corners
remove the last gluey bits of night

the house is early quiet
it's late enough to be light
early enough to be silent

I slept through Sarah's efforts
she understood about the morning escape
but won't be impressed by a dinner abandoned
being left to drink wine or eat cake on her own

*"it's like the two of you want me to get fucking fat
yee never eat and here I am stuffing my face"*

I shift across the bed, two hours until the next bus home
a rota in my head of when the bus bothers its arse stopping in Roscrea

I would drop home all the time
if home was serviced by one of those Expressways
but country towns get dismissed

I come and go at weird hours
dictated by the only bus or train
get dumped miles from where I'm going
and wait for Mammy to drive in and pick me up

at my age, she had kids, cars, mortgages
she wasn't on a bus home, a stunted adult-child
staring out the window with the guilt
of strange men gnawing at her head

I should get up, put a bag of stuff together
grab a shower, eat a nourishing breakfast

my side of the fridge, a plastic lunchbox of fermenting soup
bin-ready and pungent, some spinach gone wet with decay

the fur of my morning mouth tastes sour
I'll shower, scrub the dirt of him away
I release my hair from its tie
let its greasy lank fall around me

shower first, then I'll start to file my thoughts
arrange the day in an approachable manner

shuffle across the room
select a has-been towel from the cupboard
a scratchy reminder to replace the old
with newer, softer ways of living

there's the drill of my phone vibrating
from where I dumped my bag on the floor
a light winking out of the dark hole
where the zip is left slightly open
I check the phone, it's Edi

"what time are you headed home"

'not yet, got to
shower first
feel gross'

"you weren't out late again
were you"

I'll reply later
I can't be dealing with anti-alcohol sermons

Edi only sees Daddy
whispering to the bottom of a wine glass
about how much he loved us all

oh SHIT the pill
the most frequent of my morning thoughts
and yet, it could do with being more consistent
I reach into the bedside drawer, find a discarded green sock
shudder at where it came from, under it are condoms
owning them informs so many of my decisions
when the box runs out, I'll let it slide
then I'll be forced to blink

wait, wait, wait
did you not bring one

all shy girl, all relationship material

behind them, the card of pills
I face the days I've missed

I'll swallow them all
worry about hormonal overdose
resulting in self-induced menopause
or a baby with too many thoughts
that climbs up curtains and refuses to sit down

three in a row
that's not how pills are prescribed
I must ingest at an exact time

every

single

day

as if all days are created equal
as if anyone can maintain a predictable routine

oh, shut up head

they slide down my throat
one sticks, not enough saliva
I swallow again, it gives in and goes

mother nature will be kicking me in the ovaries
by Monday I'll be tender-headed
a change from whatever creature I am now
this dark and cranky morning beast

if I'm going to leave, it should be soon
before I've to go through the motions
of explaining him to myself or Sarah
before I find a piece of him lurking
a chapstick or chewing gum lying in my room
some corner Sarah forgot to clean
though, lord knows, she's thorough

Sarah has three sponges in the kitchen
each with a specific purpose

*"I'm like so OCD about this shit
it would be so much worse if I wasn't"*

it wouldn't, we could scrub counters
without asking a sponge *will I regret using you*
a question better spent on the men I drag home

*

I run the tap, mouth first
I can still imagine the shape of his tongue
slithering between teeth, a biter and a shover
the kind of kiss that hangs around longer than its owner
repeating over and over *do you like that bitch*

that's my type
humdingers, dickswingers

I switch the shower on
let the cold water run its course
paste my brush
scrub too hard and fast
froth gummy with red
spit and rinse and gargle
repeat, repeat, repeat
the routines that add up to a day
a comfort in rolling from bed
*clean, eat, scratch, sigh
yawn, shiver, breathe*
these are quiet mercies
before life starts in on me again

Edi says

"listen to your inner voice"

but mine is too disturbing

the shower is foggy warm, finally
step in, hold my face under the stream
it floods my eyes, skis off my nose
beneath its gush, I feel more human
as if the hours are moving backwards

I can wash it all off
lather the soap along my body
slide it over rough knees, smooth thighs
places he touched, scrub the shoulder he gripped
the hot of his breath in my head
along the left side of my neck
tickling my ear

I stare at my body blotchy with heat
shadow of stubble poking its ugly head
out of all my crevices, a hair or two stick out
around my nipple, on my stomach a trail
the cluster of dark where my body dips inwards

shave off every bit of hair
arms, legs, places I would never admit to
hairs stand on my toes, ugly hobbit clubs
blood bubbles up where I nick the skin
slides away in the water

my skin will itch and bite
I can live with that
not this dirty woman of a body

the first book I saw on puberty had a page on pubic hair
at ten, I traced the lineage of hair that would grow
the awful tufts, I cried over it, I'd had no clue
women do such a good job of hiding it

I wish to be the kind of girl
that doesn't strip away at herself
but I've grown into this shame
each day, I come back to
my pathetic horrors

after I'm done
scrubbing, rubbing, shaving, warring
I cry

some sing in showers
but I cry so I can start again

if anyone asks
I've a canned excuse
shampoo in my eye

it's hard to get out of a shower
every thought streams down into the drain
a warm and constant rain
soft pressure on my head
let go, let go, let go

I'm here too long, legs and arms
red wrinkles of their former selves

out, into the cold tiled room
I rub clear a patch of mirror
my fresh pink face
leans in and smiles

2

thirty minutes until the bus leaves
I dilly-dally on lethargic roads
weighted by a bag on my back
another strapped across me
it bumps my side with each step

sports enthusiasts, in and out of cars
backseats full of boots, muck

I'd be among them, up and down windy trails
but I'm headed home to empty roads, longer hills
the dog straining at my heel

I'll cut through Phoenix Park, light and leafy
I peep into the corner shops by the gate
one a grey square with a line of milk cartons in the fridge
the headlines of newspapers coated in politicians raving

the other, a trove of random bits and bobs
tins of soup, cake ingredients, handmade Polish biscuits
a hula hoop on a good day, chocolate on a bad

Sarah and I send Diarmaid there
to fetch the sugar we're resisting

*"but you know you're going to fucking want it
would you not just get it on the way home"*

Sarah tuts

"where's the craic in that"

that's usually the end of it
he returns laden with
more than we ask for

later, we blame him

"if you hadn't bought all those stupid sweets"

as teenagers, Edi and I
would walk three miles to the nearest shop
down Tipperary roads, cars swerved
we spent half the time in the ditch
politely waving at mildly familiar faces
to get to a dingy petrol station
where rough kids from school smoked
we crept past them to the shelves of treats
embarrassed by our cobbled-together country clothes
never up to the scratch of townie uniforms
belly-tops and flares would have set the neighbours off

"sure, where would you be going with yourself
dressed up to the nines, isn't it only the petrol station
I'll tell you this, it's not me you're trying to impress
pregnant by sixteen, mark my words"

living down a boreen meant we knew our place
trekked out in jeans and fleeces
coated in hairs from sitting on the couch
a fat cat purring on our chests
we would only notice the cat hairs
when the eyes of a townie fell on us

our return home would feel eternal
backpacks full of Maryland cookies

we learnt the art of feeding hurt from Mammy
when sad she rubbed butter into thick brown sugar
made lemon drizzle shortbread

*

now the park, the careful shape of the gates
I cut left, *down, down, down*

it's steep, a runner comes toward me
my foot catches and the tarmac hits
I land on all fours, knees, elbows grazing
sprawled, a mess of bag and girl and coat

I'm wearing terrible knickers
a polka dotted granny-size would be a blessing
I lie strangled by a lycra strip of thong

thoughts a jumble
am I hurt, make this end, oh god
oh no, oh why, get up, fat slut, tuck in
retain some fucking semblance of decency

the runner doubles back

"are you okay"

'I'm fine'

I want to say
I'm not usually like this

but he is gone
switched back
into his stride

I should have sat a minute, let him pick me up
dust me off, his good deed for the day

instead, he bounds off
wishing he hadn't bothered

3

Heuston station is pregnant with people
moving in and out of its arches
old and young, suitcases, umbrellas,
every kind of person queuing and waiting
I go through it for the sense of occasion

in all those films
love happens at train stations
people lunging across platforms
chasing each other down tracks
arms reaching out and out and out
towards those already disappearing

the Irish version is mumbled conversations
our speciality, the knowing look
only the teenagers are different
high ponytails, eyeliner, squealing
hugging beyond the cultural point of comfort

I queue beside a display of dry sandwiches
manky tuna, chicken, plastic cheese, all pre-packaged
the pastry is no more appetising
but the glaze promises to kick you awake
even if it tastes like cardboard dipped in sugar
even if I'm already picturing the lump of lard
depositing itself in the corner of some artery

"what can I get you"

the woman at the till is bored by her own question

I want to say
I work in a place like this too
I get the boredom, it eats me up

'a *latte* please
and a *pain au chocolat*'

my head cringes
don't judge me

I almost expect her to sneer or laugh out
would you go away with your latte
you're barely making rent

she'd be right, I'm head to toe discount clothing
ends of month mean beans and waffles

today, I've enough for this
surely that is all that matters
I can be careful in my thirties

some age when I'm full of the virtues of pensions
or take out a mortgage big enough to crush me

right now, I'm defined as *temporary*
any day, I could be shuffled elsewhere
I might be signing on the dole

I wait for my order, service is slow
there is a group of us pushed to one side
when an order lands, the wrong person jolts forward

we all go

"no no no"

the culprit

"oh god, I'm sorry"

such a civilised interaction
am I the only one to place importance
on a moment so insignificant

as children, the odd time we ate out
it was a fuss, Daddy detailing our three choices
from the affordable part of the menu

telling us about his granny
who used to swipe the cutlery
stuff wine glasses in her handbag
brazenly ignoring the chink and clink

my parents didn't drink *lattes*, oh no
their coffees were from petrol stations
crappy jolts of caffeine or sticks of gum
to keep them awake at the wheel

a purposefulness behind each purchase
not simply buying things to fill the time

*

I saunter through the station
pressing the coffee to my lips
sipping at hot milk-froth

this place has an echo, an actual echo
(not the disturbing metaphorical kind)
a home-grown repetition of its sounds
so we can really hear ourselves

goodbye, hello, god bless, would ye look at ye
the occasional *sláinte, it's been ages, jaysus*

I love best the silent greeters
the old man, see his flat cap
and careful leather satchel
a farmer dressed for the city
he heads toward a probable daughter
gives her one slow smiling nod
she grins and shakes her head

"I never thought I'd see the day"

they leave
fathers and daughters
how many ways a father can exist

a lump in my throat
a pain in my head

4

the bus is cramped and full

a child sits up ahead
the lights flicker on purple runners
as she kicks against the seat
she pulls a toy through the air
makes it stomp around the seat

"look, look, Mummy
it's a customisable pony"

customisable catches, that c-word
her mouth pronouncing it makes me feel
like she dug cunt out of the dictionary

the bus grinds on full of chatter
I cut to my phone, escape inside

a network full and brimming with all our empty gestures
here we go, a picture of Edi pressed up against a friend
Edi hates photos, but people want her in them
her smile is split open and people are liking it like crazy
they can't see how much she doesn't want to be there

"soooooo pretty"

"stunning babes"

despite hating to be called babes
she has thumbed-up all the comments

scroll, scroll, scroll
past babies and gloating
people sharing long, long, long statuses
I half-read these essays, make sure to like them
so they feel like someone is listening

two older ladies sit in front of me
locked in conversation

one has the soft shape of someone
who gave her body up for others
the other seems sad and savage
until she says

*"for feck's sake, she's seventy-three
is she ever going to stop doing so much
and take a bit of care of herself"*

this is it
when will any of us ever stop
and take a bit of care of ourselves

I distract myself with the bus window
the landscape shifts to familiar territory
grey gives way to green, postcard country

my phone's constant pull
the red of notifications
read me, read me, read me

I scroll past someone's breakfast, flat-looking eggs
followed by the death of a granny
someone else downs a cocktail
eyes not quite meeting the camera

*dead eggs
dead granny
dead eyes*

all in a little row

after all that death, a bit of life
bikini poses, grinning hard at cameras
landing on our feeds halfway across the world

click in, so thin, have they always been so skinny
I stare for too long at the lines on their stomachs
underneath someone comments

"that thigh gap though"

a girl from my year poses with her baby
how is she collected enough to mother
how do I get to that from this

shush, brain, shush

I don't need a baby, none of us do
I'm part of the new generation of women
meant for careers and yoga retreats
and long, long therapy sessions
where we express our childhoods
blame our parents for being human

if only my life was photogenic
what can I post
hey guys, headed home
to what, my granny's party
where Mammy's sisters will pretend to be close
until Mary jokes about Cathy's burnt soup

"it was one fucking time
will you ever let me forget"

I could post pictures of each of my parents
hovering at opposite ends of the room
pretending not to know the other is there

or comment, glibly, *odds of ten to one that Edi will cry*
perhaps at 11 pm or 4 am, before threatening to leave

she'll say

"I shouldn't have come
it's always the same"

she'll mean it, suitcase ready
two miles down the road at Mammy's house
perched in anticipation
it will be easy to gather what's scattered
mascara, powder
she is prepared to leave at a moment's notice

I'll coax her down
suggest we go home, along dark roads
we'll bitch like we always do
about what we cannot forget

when we land back in the cold cottage
she'll unpack, curl up on her bed

"it's not that bad, let's go in the morning"

if I had any gumption
I'd be ready to leave with her
grab her hand and say
we are going home

over and over and over
until one of us figures out where that is

*

it's Granny's fault
she invites him to parties
Mammy makes soft protests
but Granny is firm

"you made your bed, aren't you lucky enough to get out of it
he was part of my life too, you can't expect me to let him go"

what she means is it wouldn't be proper, not to the outskirt peepers
the cross-carrying, Hail Mary wheelers and dealers
for Granny, marriage was a vow of silence

"sure we all have our problems"

after the divorce, Granny sent letters to *Mrs Martin Lavelle*
using his name to remind my mother of her sins

Mammy, intent on becoming herself
refused to answer to names that weren't on her birth cert

after nineteen years, she wanted herself back
woke one day, so certain of it, that we knew just looking at her
when she stopped the car on the side of the road
we understood before the words came out

"I'm leaving your father"

and Edi from the backseat

"finally"

that year transformed my mother
the last cruelty was insignificant
yet suddenly she knew
no more, no more, no more

an upside-down year for us, but how was it for her
the nights she found sleep, only to wake in a cold sweat
stomach tight and nervous

that Christmas, I brought home a CD

'you should listen to this'

the Pogues played *A Rainy Night in Soho*
a song I didn't know my mother loved
she faced out the window, into the black sky
tears rolling down her cheeks
the words filled every inch of the room

*"I've been loving you a long time
down all the years, down all the days
and I've cried for all your troubles
smiled at your funny little ways"*

part of her still loved him

5

the bus slows around roundabouts
hefts its weight along narrow town roads
squeezes to a halt by Roscrea castle
two of us get up, me and a lad dressed like the GAA
my bags brush off other passengers

"sorry, sorry, sorry"

the driver has a thick slab of accent

"mind yerself"

'thanks'

he smiles

"no bother
any bags below"

'I don't
thanks'

no need to activate the buses hymn
luggage doors operating

the road is emptyish, ten poorly-parked cars
I never thought I'd like this uncertain place
the shop where they lost the *o* in *euro*
tacked on a different sized font
the beaten-up signs of other stores

Mammy is parked a few cars down
sitting, head down, book resting on the wheel
half here and half in some fictitious world
her mind forever traipsing into Georgian houses
and sitting down to tea in long silks

she looks up, smile big
(somehow, she knew I was watching)
swings open the door, hops out

I forget how small she is
she comes towards me, then halts
murmurs some half-formed apology

'how long have
you been waiting'

I want to sit on the ground and say
I give up, I cannot be grown-up
can I come home and light the fires
I'll mind you, cook the dinners, clean
and read books, we can discuss that time
until we've exorcised him from our lives

my voice is colder than I intend

'you should have waited
for me to text'

"I only just got here"

I let it slide
no point in arguing

we hug, it is good to feel her arms around me
scent of Oil of Olay cream
and good old-fashioned soap

we sit into the car
wait for Edi's bus

the car is manky from a recent hiking trip
there's branches on the seat beside me

"shove those to one side"

she acts unsure of how they got there
she's full of stories about a farmer down the road
who has taken to dropping off wheelbarrows of manure
the odd uplifting bag of home-grown cabbage

the bus arrives, people pile down
Edi is the last out, she looks different

her body shifts across the months
when she is round, skin blotched
no ugly part of me feels inadequate

but today, her hair is soft and permed
jeans sag slightly, a deep green top skims
inwards with the line of her stomach
she's thinner than me

an awkward wave at us
she bends to retrieve her bag
from the bus's dark mouth

"I'm so excited"

grin genuine

'excited about what'

it comes out wrong
with the disjointing sound of anger

Edi ignores me
flicks the radio to Spin Southwest
Justin Bieber blares, *it's too late now to say sorry*
windows fog, Edi sings along, shoulder slides

I want to say
this isn't going to be much fun
this bit now is fine, the car and catch-up
but we will run out of harmless words
grow irritated by what we haven't changed
start blaming each other for loving him

Edi builds us up inside her head
remembers us as if
we are still tucked up with Mammy
each wrapped in one of her arms
limpets, as she read *Harry Potter* in bed
our heads lit up with other worlds

he hid that book
he didn't want us having a place to go

Edi always says that Mammy made places anyway
hedgerow cubbies, rainy-day mattress forts
Saturday library trips, long forest hikes
pens and paper for drawing or writing
old boxes folded into dragons

and now, she pre-scripts weekends
as if we're all still part of that world

⋆

"I've to pop into Tesco"

we park in the closet of a carpark
ascend into bright commercial air

Mammy takes the stairs
we lounge on the flat escalator
laughing at her hurried steps
she bounds up the stairs, two at a time
to prove the old way is better

marching to the baskets
triumphantly reaching them before us
a pink glow to her cheeks, breath short

*"didn't I tell you the stairs are quicker
and it keeps me fit"*

'you nearly
took out that child
lunging up them
like that'

"what child"

she asks, alarmed

there's not a lot of people here
not like Dublin, where shops are full of women in nice clothes
contemplating the repercussions of calories
here, baskets brim with carrots, Brennan's bread, eggs, milk
Dublin baskets would be full of quinoa, avocados and hummus
as if we've all forgotten where we come from

women man the checkouts, once-crisp uniforms wilted
processed hair, bad skin, taking customer care seriously
forcing out facts about the weather with old ladies

"it's three degrees warmer than this time last year
we'll get a fine summer if it keeps this up"

in the city, they'd beep through items, sigh

first stop, vegetable aisle

'what do you have
in the house'

Mammy rifles through the empty fridge in her mind

"not much"

Edi grabs her own basket
we fill it with the food we eat
we don't ask if it hurts her
only assume we're helping

Mammy places yoghurts in a separate basket
not letting us get away with it fully

since we left home, her brimming larder has faltered
we find half a bag of spinach, an egg, some cheese
a potato half rotting in a drawer, stale bread for toasting

her excuse

"I'm not that hungry by myself"

she grew up in a big family
moved out to a big family
grew herself a family
she's never eaten alone
it takes getting used to
a silent room
the sound of your own chewing

as kids, she would not let us eat alone
breakfasts, dinners, lunches, were all occasions
flowery jugs for milk, pottery plates for Sundays
silver cutlery and colourful teapots
she baked buns or cakes once a week
every day the dinner was different

"sure, you couldn't be facing
the same food two days running"

for eighteen years, she filled our stomachs
with Moroccan spices, Indonesian dishes
her kitchen shelf home to fifty cook books
on Saturdays, we leafed through them
to decide what miracle of food to create

and now, she picks at half-empty bowls

*

we glide through aisles
filling our baskets

Mammy says

"I won't finish all that
you're only here for a day"

Edi laughs

"you wouldn't want us going hungry"

a trick we learnt from our father
the only way to get around her
lay the guilt on thick and heavy

6

our cottage is less leafy in autumn
I haven't been home since August
blanket smoothed-out, lumpy grass
cups of tea, books in laps

now, the grey September light has made it wet and dark
ivy grows around the windows

our childhood cottage was smothered
by trellises of clematis
once a year, Daddy scalped them
leaving the cottage naked
so, nature knew not to mess with him

I unfurl from the car, Mammy juggles keys
nods towards a potted plant

"it's been a hard year for them"

Edi and I roll eyes, voice a polite

"sure isn't that terrible"

we never got our heads around the garden gene

I breathe in the grass, mud, nearby tractors
pot-holed roads and bramble-lined ditches
the dog scoots around to paw me
slides his tongue along my hand
I curl it back, hating the warm rot of dog breath
the rough wet texture of his tongue

I can't remember his name, there've been so many
scraped up off the road, or injected at the vets
taken out back with the rifle

dogs go missing, no sense in getting attached
he could be Sam or Kirk or Gumbo
I pat his head, murmur

'good boy'

maleness is a quality Mammy's dogs have
she is careful about females

"she'll only go getting herself pregnant"

as kids, we'd watch her hold puppies and kittens to the light
dividing them into piles of males and females
she let us choose from the boys
sometimes, she'd get the gender wrong
we'd end up with a pregnant cat or dog

and curse it

*

*"throw your bags up in the room girls
I'll get the fire on"*

it's dimly lit, the cold of stone
Mammy is already at the fire
briquettes, firelighters, wood
the complications of warmth

she points at hot water bottles
perched by the kettle
we boil and pour water in
screw the stoppers on
tuck them under our jumpers

I grew up in cold like this
but accustomed to city living
it gets right into me
no boost button here
or hot water waiting in the tap

we traipse upstairs, claim the beds
she keeps perfectly made for us
ghost beds fitted with matching quilts
heirlooms of our past
shelves groan with the Famous Five
old Leaving Cert books and trinkets

"will we go down
and help"

I ask, before the time warp swallows me
and I end up at the bottom of some box
gooing and gahing over notes
we once pressed under each other's doors
back when Daddy banned us
from spending too much time together

downstairs
Mammy checks the clock

"we'll have a bite to eat
Edi could do with a bit of food"

Edi gets dizzy from lights or loud noises
her legs weak and no longer able to move

we pile the table with cheese, crackers
fruit, juice, homemade chutneys
sit, nibble, chat

the hours go quickly
halfway through a pot of tea
we spread out across the house to get ready

when we're all plucked, showered
smoothed over and mascaraed
we re-congregate

Edi is wearing a red dress, a velvet shimmer
it sits on her just right

Mammy is in a purple clingy number
that makes her uncomfortable
the dress would suit her fine
if she wore it like she meant it

but there's the prickle of him
in the back of her mind
he will stand across a room
mind-hissing

slut   slut   slut

so vehemently
we can already hear it

7

before we leave
Mammy takes two beers from the fridge

"I'll need more than alcohol-free crap tonight"

as if 500 ml of alcohol might scoot her over the edge
allow her to dance across the rooftop of her childhood
I suggested tequila, Edi winced

"would it be easier to not go"

'oh yeah, cos Granny is famed
for her understanding'

*

the road glistens in the lights of passing cars

I suck in the sky, how lovely it is
I want it to mean more to me than *lovely*
so many lives dedicated to finding meaning
in the stars and lines of planets
the fullness of the moon

Edi, stuck in the same thought asks

"can you name any of them"

hand gesturing at the stars
Mammy looks up

*"there, there is the North Star
and if you pay attention the Plough"*

she traces the outline with her torch
beam stretching out to join the dots

"wow, that's one powerful torch"

more impressed by man-made tools
than the universe spread above us
we fall into our separate thoughts

a man once showed me Venus

*"it's the brightest star in the sky
and it's not even a star"*

when I half-replied, he said

*"you're the only person I've met
that doesn't get how cool that is"*

scared by my inadequacy
I kissed him hard

I was not surprised
to find him gone the next morning
since then, I've tried to look at stars
and really see them

*

Mammy quietens as we near the house
the trees she climbed across as a child
the boggy fields she ran through

we're greeted by a half-arsed line of cars
most of them parked parallel to the ditch
the odd one left in a disgruntled hurry
lopsided and jutting out into the road

mostly bangers
battered by bad roads
L plates on many of them
Baby on Board stuck to back windows

the red tips of cigarette smokers
puffing under the porch awning
one or two aunts, but mostly the young
the old have had years tight enough to make them quit

a man with an ashy kiss
once told me

*"it gives me a purpose
when I feel awkward"*

he took another drag
I wondered was it true of everyone
the hardest task is to sit and be

I don't smoke, but I'm as bad
at parties I help in the kitchen
squash myself between women
who've earned their place at the sink
bolster myself, insist on scrubbing dishes
pretend to love cleaning
*oh, wire brushes, sponges, suds
the stuff of dreams*

*

Granny's house looks older
plants growing stray, a line of bushes forming one long ratty hedge
the cars that fit in the yard are parked half in and out of patchy gravel

key in the front door lock

*"sure there's nothing worth stealing
they're welcome to it"*

inside, Granny's near the door
shrunk and plump
glasses perched on her nose

she tells one of the young cousins

*"I love a girl in good tight jeans
makes you want to pinch her bum"*

the cousin nods seriously, intent on being inoffensive
Granny laughs so loud it becomes a hoarse and rasping cough
she spots us at the door, mutters what sounds like

"young people have no sense of humour
I suppose it died with good manners"

we smile politely

Edi nudges me
she's caught sight of him in the corner
deep in chat with one of the neighbours
a community-minded man

Daddy nods across the room
we avert our eyes

Mammy fumbles about on the counter
for a gadget to open her beer

"girls, you go on ahead
I need a minute"

she ducks towards the bathroom
ready to sit there for a while
pressing a cold beer bottle to her forehead
sipping it as she gathers herself

Edi gives me a look, it says
this is going to be one long night
you better be ready to pick her up
act normal, act normal, act normal

Edi is good at parties
wide smile full of questions
sitting, listening, stepping between groups
laughing at bad impersonations
remembering each development
Uncle William's snowdrop collection
or that Aunty Cathy went back to work last month

I sit in a chair from the seventies
stained wood with paint flecks
from when the kitchen was refinished

our aunties stand by the fire bitching
it's clear from the heads on them
bent in, going hard at it
it's always the same, soon
they will turn on each other

Granny's house is big
she only uses the front of it
cluttered with people

books and pots of jam dot every surface
the party spread between sitting room and kitchen
two rooms that ache with cold, unless full, like now
with people we have always known
and in another way, do not know at all

our uncles, big kind men, stop to ask about Daddy
check I'm holding up okay
as if he's not sitting on the low couch
chatting to distant cousins
the ones that are shady on the details

Uncle Cormac, a corner shrinker
latches on to people at the edges
to divulge his latest conspiracy theory

Mammy says

"he's grand
until you get stuck listening to him"

as if by way of explanation
the family shake their head at his name

"the recession was hard on him"

not suited to the modern workplace
when others went back to schoolbooks
he holed up, said he'd wait it out
he types with one finger
never quite recovered from IKEA
pushing him out of business

his kids don't come to parties anymore
we stopped asking why two years ago

Cormac has cornered Caroline
the kindest sister, second oldest
the one who drives Granny to Mass
buys her vegetables and checks in
drops up dinner when Granny's ill

she endures his rant on politics

"the money for NAMA, where did that go
the farms, yeah, it's good for the farms
but how much farmland is there and how much fishland
them farms are only a drop in the ocean of what we've lost
and it's our own fault, it's not Europe that's different, it's us"

Aunty Mary appears at my side

"Beth, is that you
I can hardly tell the difference anymore"

'I didn't see you there
you're looking well, lovely dress'

"oh I've had it years
I just stuck it on"

she starts in on boyfriends
the puzzled lip purse
at no significant other

maybe she's a lesbian
scurrying through her mind
Mammy says they get it from Granny
who would tell them

"I've the right to know who I've raised"

Mary wants to do the same, refrains
I almost tell her what it's like
but it's too complicated

imagine explaining
the no-strings-attached nature of dating

I could say
well I can gift you stories, do you want guy three or six
cos both of those Mary
they were shining examples of testosterone
one was a solicitor, a nice firm job
the kind of career that wives get spending money on
if you can figure out how to snag one, email me
I've only worked out the getting them into bed bit
how did you get yours to stay

her husband is a signed blank cheque
(we choose our sacrifices)
she wakes up beside a man
who laughs at fart jokes

'nobody special yet'

I say *yet*
as if it might change
any minute now
I'll pull one out of a hat

Mary moves on to office life

"you shouldn't do anything you don't love"

that's her take on existence
and yet she does her husband

"are you liking work at the minute
your mum said you're finding it tough"

I'm about to answer
Granny rushes towards me
voice urgent

"I need help with the sandwiches
nobody is eating them"

'maybe they're
not hungry'

nobody ever comes here peckish
we've all grown up with Granny saying
cleaning pans is pointless

"you lose all the flavour"

her kitchen is an experiment in flavour development
every surface covered with a plant or a trowel caked in mud

some days, half way through gardening
she remembers there's food to eat
potters in, grabs whatever is going
as likely to gnaw on stale bread
as a fried egg specked with black from the pan

last Christmas, the cake was raw in the middle
it was one of the few staples
we could count on her Christmas cake

she shoved it in the oven
took the time to cook it right
lovingly rolled out the marzipan
pasted on thick royal icing

but this time, she took it from the oven early
the egg, still raw, went slowly rancid

we sat around, sneaking lumps into the fire

Edi, polite as ever, swallowed it down
lump after rotting lump
she spent a day in bed

Caroline was sent to dispose of the cake
the text fired across family WhatsApp

"nobody eat the cake"

Granny found out, indignant

she ate a slice to prove it was fine
ended up under blankets for ten days

(at least she didn't die
imagine writing cause of death as Christmas cake)

Granny leads me to the kitchen
counters stacked with plates of cling-filmed sandwiches
Granny's labelled them with a black permanent marker
the ink misshapen across the lumps and bumps
beetroot and tuna, egg salad
ham & cheese, pickles & cheese, pot-luck
she must have been up all night
slicing and pressing them together

I circle the two rooms
hand them to reluctant relatives
who chew with a smile
look at Granny

(who is watching from the corner)

"how lovely"

smiles disappearing
as teeth catch on a bit of grit or hair

*

there's no avoiding him
he's sitting to my right

I hold the sandwiches firmly between us

'would you like one Daddy'

"of course, how are you Beth"

he asks in a sad whimper

'I'm fine'

he looks at me
as if to assess the damage
and says carefully

"I'm glad to hear it"

everyone strains to hear
there's a quiet lull of voices
the lean-in of their ears

have they invited him just to see what happens
if they shove us all in a room together

'are you in the old house'

though I know well he'll live there for as long as he can
across the fields, raking in the pity
abandoned in the cottage of his marriage

"I am, you should come by
I've kept your room"

which is to say he's left it empty
I boxed up every bit of me
no books or teddies lounge
waiting for me to reclaim them

'I will'

I'm lying
this is an old act
we recite it elegantly

"bring Edi
I'll cook your favourite"

I want to say
you don't know my favourite food
shut your goddamn sanctimonious face
you've already taken all I had to give you

'that would be nice'

I wince
he's about to pry further
when Aunty Mary steps in

*"Beth hand out those sandwiches before we starve
or Granny has a hernia over the waste
sorry Martin, I'm sure you understand"*

*"not to worry Mary
duty calls"*

he says as the smile slides off his face
Mary lost my mother to him for nineteen years
was quick to take her back when it was all over
on sad nights, she brought wine bottles and belly laughs
but there's too much lost between them
to fit comfortably into their old roles

I shrug, as if to explain
*I'd stay, but there's a pressing demand
for fermenting beetroot sandwiches*
I pass the food out

Mammy is still missing
she disappears at parties
curls up in her mother's room reading
or I might find her out in the garden
cold breath visible as she charges after children
asks Granny about the roses

I pawn the sandwiches off on one of the younger cousins

I say, to nobody really

'I'll nip to the bathroom'

the air in the hall is cold and damp
two of the youngest cousins flood past
screaming into the yard

"they're coming, they're coming"

it takes a moment to remember who they are
there's so many of us and we see each other so little

I brush aside the dumped coats
open the cupboard under the stairs
and sit inside, closing the door behind me

I've sat here a thousand times
cushioned by a wicker basket
full of lampshades Granny gave up on
the slanted ceiling above me

outside, the laughing and clinking
I sit and breathe a minute
prepare myself to face him

I focus on the contents of the cupboard
a rolled-up carpet maroon and patterned
a map of Ireland from before maps were accurate
old coats and hats growing fat with dust
crutches from a farmyard accident
the nozzle of a hoover

how many have come in here
sat on this floor between the boxes

damn, this girlish habit of hiding
I've always crawled into tight spaces
lain under mattresses, pressed against springs
listened to my name flying between rooms

"Beth, Beth, Beth"

I'd hold my knees to my chest
heart whispering

I'm not here, not yet
let silence grow in me
the cold comes with it
numb feet and hands

I'm about to leave

when footsteps stop and move towards me
the door opens and Edi steps in

"I knew I'd find you here"

she sits into the basket
body dipping against the lampshades

*"we're going soon, Mammy can't do it
did you see the state of him"*

I nod, by *state* she means
how carefully he maintained calm

sandwiched back together
off on whispered Daddy tangents

'and he was all over Cormac
agreeing with him about NAMA
he gives literally no shits about NAMA'

I listen to myself, as if I'm someone else
the conversation punctuated by him
we make ourselves his endless victims

my heart is too withered for this
we remember childhood differently

"it was more like this"

'no, *I* said that'

"you always give yourself the best bits of the story"

tales grow scalier and stranger with age
we fall upon some other cruelty, spit him out
here we are, raking over the old dirt
as if we never left our common ground

it's in the set of Edi's shoulders
she can't do it this time either

we don't want to end up in undecided territory
bickering over who said what and when

*

Mammy is not in Granny's room or the garden

Edi asks

"should we check the upstairs"

'she wouldn't go up there'

"maybe she went back in"

*

that's exactly where she is
ten metres from him
back to the fire, warming her hands

Caroline beside her, not speaking, standing
letting her solid aura keep Mammy firm
we ask how life is going

"oh, the same old, same old"

I want to grow old like Caroline
soft and gentle despite life
standing close to my sister on bad nights
bolstering her when she needs it

Daddy's eyes are on us

I give a bland salute in his direction
he nods back and I'm sure he chalks this up as a victory
his mind a meticulous spreadsheet, keeping score of all encounters

maybe not, maybe this is all me
I could be the only one keeping tabs

in the beginning, Mammy told us to visit him

"it's good to see your father
you'll regret it if you don't"

she bit her lip when we ranted
scared of manipulating us

on the third weekend visit, his car arrived to take us
to an expensive lunch, like he was wooing us

he hopped out of the car
administered perfunctory hugs on the side of the road
in case the neighbours were paying attention

Edi said to him

"I need to talk to you"

she had not warned me this was coming
his arms went loose, he walked quickly to the car
closed himself in and locked the doors
sat with his hands on the wheel
staring straight ahead

he was shaking, so was Edi

she stepped around, tapped his window
said again

"we need to talk"

he didn't flinch
eyes fixed on another space and time

Edi continued
at first low, then shouting

"I can't do this stuff, after what you've done to us
I don't want your expensive dinners or birthday presents
I won't be bought off like that and I'm not going to be
I'm not sure we should see each other any more"

her voice cut up the boreen
she was only sixteen

"I should have known you'd act like this"

turning on her heel
she went back inside the house
leaving me to wonder
where did she get all that strength

I stood behind the car, wanting to follow
slowly he rolled down the window

"and what about you
are you coming"

I sat into the car, we went to a castle
I spoke, mouth-dry, about college-plans
ate a cheese board, spilled the tea
and the cheese clung to the guilt
pounding the walls of my arteries

before Mammy left him
it was us against them
then us against Daddy
now, it was just me

I sat alone with him
Edi had given up on me
or I on her

I can't tell anymore

when he dropped me home
he folded a fifty euro note into my hand
if only there was enough of me
to throw it back in his face

I'm the one that's never tackled him
despite all my bawdy bitching

the night she said divorce
he said

"Beth, you'll keep us together
we're a family
even if your mother wants to break us"

*

now, he aims a smile at me
I could go over to him

but I'm done shrinking

instead, I hold his gaze
until he's the one
who has to look away

Edi catches the exchange, murmurs

"would he ever just give it a rest"

Mammy smiles as if to say
it's okay girls, we're the bigger people

this is my cue to say I'm tired
to suggest we leave as a united front

instead, I let them fall back into conversation
Edi laughs at something Mammy says

I move away, nobody notices
I do not offer up a single goodbye
no excuses, no hugs, no backward glances

out the door, I step into the night

8

pitch dark, my senses lead me along the pot-holed road
past cars and homes and people I've known my whole life
I throw myself into it, heart tight and pounding in my chest
each sharp breath a reminder of how much it hurts to feel
each footstep brings me back to earth

tomorrow, I will call him
voice cracking down the line
enough, enough, enough

until he hears me
until he hangs up

I note the trees, thin and skeletal
against the dark and blotted sky

I pick up the pace
oh night sky, oh winding road

ALVY CARRAGHER is an Irish poet and writer based in Toronto. She has published two books. Her first collection of poetry *Falling in love with broken things* was published in 2016 by Salmon Poetry and her children's novel *The Cantankerous Molly Darling* was published in 2019. She received first-class honours in her MA of Writing from the National University of Ireland, Galway. As a performance poet, she featured at events like Electric Picnic, Edinburgh Fringe Fest, RTE's Arena and the Cúirt International Literary Festival. Shc represented Poetry Ireland at a reading in the Lincoln Center, New York as part of the Poetry Ireland Introduction Series in 2016. You can find out more about her work at www.alvycarragher.com

salmonpoetry

Cliffs of Moher, County Clare, Ireland

"Like the sea-run Steelhead salmon that thrashes upstream to its spawning ground, then instead of dying, returns to the sea—Salmon Poetry Press brings precious cargo to both Ireland and America in the poetry it publishes, then carries that select work to its readership against incalculable odds."

TESS GALLAGHER

BEING DRAGGED ACROSS THE CARPET BY THE CAT

Dónall Dempsey

"Does the soul find herself or not? The soul finds herself in the point where every rational being understands itself by itself."

- Meister Eckhart

First Edition July 2013

Published by Dempsey&Windle

ISBN: 9781907435157

Available from
http://www.lulu.com/spotlight/JanWindle66

Other books by Dónall Dempsey:

Sifting Sound into Shape

Wordless Book